WW1 CENTENARY ART COMMISSIONS

Fashion &
Freedom

Manchester Art Gallery

"Fashion is often dismissed as a frivolous thing, but in reality it is interwoven into our social and political history. This is why it is so crucial to tell this story at this important moment and demonstrate the powerful and vital role fashion continues to play."

Caroline Rush CBE, CEO British Fashion Council

Fashion & Freedom is co-commissioned by Manchester Art Gallery and 14-18 NOW: WW1 Centenary Art Commissions, supported by the National Lottery through the Heritage Lottery Fund and Arts Council England, and by the Department for Culture Media and Sport

Contents

Foreword

Perhaps it's unsurprising that most exhibitions about the First World War focus on the impact it had on the male population, and especially on the young men who fought in it. By contrast, this exhibition looks at the often-neglected but profound effect that the war had on the lives of British women, and particularly the way it helped to advance their campaign for wider freedoms.

The mass exodus of men to the battlefields during the war gave British women the chance and sometimes the obligation to try new roles and take on new responsibilities. With these jobs came a need for new clothing: freer, looser and more practical. This contributed to the evolution of modern fashion, a lasting impact which we still recognise today. Women's activities during wartime also helped their fight for the right to vote, a vital freedom that some of them won just as the war ended in 1918.

With a fascinating mix of historic dress and newly commissioned pieces, this exhibition celebrates the new fashions and freedoms that were worn and won by women in 1914-18. Leading designers and film-makers have produced some unmissable new work that brings to life this amazing story. And more than 200 students at British fashion colleges have been looking ahead to the next innovations in fashion by paying homage to the revolutions of 100 years ago.

Fashion & Freedom is part of 14-18 NOW, a five-year programme of extraordinary arts experiences connecting people with the First World War. We are delighted to be working with Manchester Art Gallery and other inspirational partners across the UK to commission and present a wide range of new works from leading contemporary artists, works that take a fresh look at the events of 1914-18 and their impact on our world today. You can discover more about our programme at 1418NOW.org.uk.

Jenny Waldman
Director, 14-18 NOW: WW1 Centenary Art Commissions

Foreword

Fashion & Freedom sees today's leading female fashion designers and exceptional filmmakers explore the impact that the First World War had on the changing role of women and fashion. Inspired by the profound changes in women's dress during the war, they have created unique commissions which are exhibited at Manchester Art Gallery. We are delighted to be working with 14-18 NOW to realise *Fashion & Freedom*, which gives our visitors a new way to understand the impact of the war through the lens of fashion.

Alongside the new commissions, this project enables us to showcase outfits from our rich costume collection. We are displaying day and evening wear from the pre-war period which reflect the strict rules about dress and Edwardian social conventions. A Women's Royal Naval Service (WRNS) uniform from the collection dating from 1918 is an example of an auxiliary military role that women undertook during the war and is influenced by masculine tailoring. The two post-war dresses from the 1920s demonstrate a new informality with a boyish silhouette and shorter hemlines. Pre and post-war outfits juxtaposed side by side reveal in stark terms these changes to women's fashion over the wartime period.

Restriction / Release is a significant part of the project which presents new work from students from five fashion colleges including two influential local fashion courses at Manchester School of Art and the University of Salford. These new works examine the two physical extremes women faced within fashion, from the tight fitted corsets of pre-war to the soft free-flowing silhouette of post-war.

It is particularly appropriate for a project about the changing role of women to launch in Manchester, the birthplace of the Suffragette movement. The home of Emmeline Pankhurst at 62 Nelson Street, Manchester, where the first meeting of the Women's Social and Political Union was held in 1903, still stands in the city today. By displaying items from our collection in dialogue with new pieces commissioned from contemporary designers and filmmakers, connections are created between the past and present.

It is a source of some shame and anger for me personally to note how much women are still judged by what they wear and how they look in 2016. This exhibition is a salutary and inspiring reminder that women have always had to fight for their autonomy and their freedom. The stunning new pieces by some of Britain's most creative designers, and the response by the students who will be the next generation of creative rule-breakers reminds us that this is a relevant battle even today.

Dr Maria Balshaw CBE
Director, Manchester City Galleries

Collection Manchester City Galleries 1947.2535

Introduction

The First World War brought immense change to women's lives. As men left home to fight on the frontline, around 1.5 million women joined the industrial workforce, taking on jobs as bus conductors, ambulance drivers and window cleaners, as well as in offices and factories. New responsibility gave women new freedom and led to a new ways of dressing as silhouettes and social codes changed. *Fashion & Freedom* reflects upon the significant changes in women's lives and fashions as a result of the war. The exhibition has been made possible by 14-18 NOW, the UK's arts programme for the First World War centenary. It brings together new commissions of contemporary fashion design and film shown alongside historic dress from Manchester Art Gallery's collection.

Leading female fashion designers Holly Fulton, Roksanda Ilincic, Jackie JS Lee, Vivienne Westwood, Emilia Wickstead and Sadie Williams have created new pieces inspired by the stories of women during wartime. Emerging designers from five universities have responded to the theme of *Restriction / Release*, reflecting on the changes to the fashionable silhouette from the Edwardian period through to the 1920s.

Original films have been commissioned that are contemporary creative reflections on the experience of women, before, during and after the First World War. These include shorts by directors from Nick Knight's award-winning SHOWstudio, who pioneered fashion film online and by Luke Snellin, whose cast wear specially designed uniforms by Manchester fashion label Private White V.C.

Fashion & Freedom explores new ways of understanding the powerful impact of the First World War and how fashion is interwoven into the social and political history of Britain. *Fashion & Freedom* showcases new creative works that echo these histories a century later.

Historic Costume

The creative commissions presented in *Fashion & Freedom* were inspired in part by fashion history before, during and after the First World War. Although many factors led to changes in fashionable dress in the first quarter of the 20th century, the war accelerated the course of fashion history. The historic pieces from Manchester's City Galleries costume collection and loans trace a brief timeline of women's fashion from the Edwardian period to the mid-1920s.

Silhouettes, fabrications and details similar to those in these historic pieces were incorporated by the contemporary designers in their works for *Fashion & Freedom*, connecting the stories and the materials of the wartime period to creative fashion design today.

Encounters with the Historic:
Dress from Manchester City Galleries' collection

There has been a public costume collection in Manchester for nearly a hundred years. The first items of dress came to the corporation in 1922 as part of a vast collection of 'bygones' assembled by the wealthy collector, Mary Greg, wife of Thomas Greg, the heir to a textile-manufacturing firm. Included amongst over 850 items were 40 dresses and many accessories and textiles, and these formed the foundation for future collecting policies and priorities in Manchester. Active collecting during the later 1930s and, oddly, during the Second World War, meant that by 1945 the Manchester Guardian could declare the collection: 'the most important public collection of the sort outside London' (Manchester Guardian, 4 October 1945).[1]

Indeed, 75 dresses were acquired in 1940 alone, perhaps representing a rush to deposit treasured heirlooms into safe hands, and one of these costumes has been selected for the exhibition as a fine representation of evening wear in the Edwardian, pre-First World War period[2]. Interestingly, this dress was donated by Mrs Alice Laycock of Scarborough, who chose Manchester as her nearest costume collection.

Manchester's costume collection became truly significant in 1947 with the successful purchase of a large private collection amassed by Drs. Cecil Willett and Phillis Cunnington. After a public appeal to raise £7,000, over 3,000 pieces were acquired, largely dating from 1760 to 1920, including a remarkable library and archive. The management of such a large donation propelled the early curators into formulating costume methodologies to catalogue, store and document the collection and these became instrumental internationally. Women's dress from 1800 to 1914 comprised the most important element of the collection, and for this section of the exhibition, a dramatic example of couture by Gaston Worth has been selected to illustrate the intricacies of Edwardian daywear for the wealthy woman.[3]

The Cunningtons were both from a medical background and described their analysis of fashion history as a 'diagnosis' based on the shaping and reshaping of the body.[4] They also looked to their clothes collection as a 'typical' selection, illustrative of mass psychology and not of individual whim or taste. Because of this, they deliberately removed the provenance from any of the pieces they were given or bought. This is now severely limiting both for research purposes and in exhibition interpretation.

However, occasionally details of the wearer have managed to survive with the garment, as with the Gaston Worth dress. Here a paper label from the House records the client (Mme Claude Watney), the Atelier (Bolio[?]) and the model number (70378). Ada Annie Nunn married Claude Watney, the heir to a brewery business, her second husband, in 1895. They were early motorcar enthusiasts and a photograph of Ada by Lafayette was published in *The Car Illustrated* in June 1902 (Figure 1).

Gaston Worth (1856-1926) was one of the two sons of the celebrated Charles Frederick Worth, seen as fashion's first

Figure 1
Mrs Claude Watney, published photograph by James Lafayette
in *The Car Illustrated*, June 1902

couturier. With his brother Jean Philippe (1853-1924), Gaston continued the management of House of Worth after Charles Frederick's death in 1895.

Edwardian fashion can be seen as the culmination of decades of increasing stylisation and elaboration during the later Victorian period. Social conventions relating to the wearing of dress had ossified, becoming deeply complicated, either for occasions such as afternoon visiting, dinner wear, evening wear, and formal ball/opera dress; or for rites of passage such as mourning or marriage. Social restrictions were mirrored in the constrictions of dress, most physically in corsetry. Manufactured corsets became ever more complex and intricate, a hidden armour re-forming the female shape and reinventing the silhouette.

Manchester has an excellent collection of over 120 pairs of stays and corsets, dating from the early 17th century onwards. Of these, 16 date to 1900-14 but only two from 1920-30. As there were no particularly striking examples for exhibition we have borrowed two pieces from the comprehensive Symington Collection, Leicestershire County Council Museum Service.

The superbly statuesque Jenyns' corset, patented in Australia in 1911, is described in its promotional booklet as 'the reducing and supporting' corset, with elaborate, pseudo-medical instructions for 'application' including a rather bizarre image of a woman strapping on her corset in 'the recumbent position'. The figure is moulded 'into fashionable lines' by the upper corset and by a novel hip-cinching belt[5] (Figure 2). Mrs E R Jenyns

THIS Corset is best applied by the wearer taking the recumbent position (as here illustrated), as by this means the abdominal viscera, which under natural conditions occupy their normal place when a person is laying down, are firmly held in such position when the Corset is adjusted, and the tissues, which are weakened or strained by any form of prolapse, have the weight and strain removed and are given an opportunity to regain their healthy strength.

And this is all done while at the same time adding a charm and grace to the figure which cannot be better obtained by any other existing make of Corset.

DIRECTIONS

This Reducing and Supporting Corset is quickly and easily applied.

First loosen the back lacings; then fasten the busks in the usual way; now fasten the suspenders; then take a belt in either hand, as shown in Fig. 1, and draw outwards until the desired shape is obtained; then bring the belt forward and snap on stud at either side, as shown in Fig. 2. Now buckle to front lappet, as shown in Fig. 3. Next draw the waist lace and tie in front. Lastly, the top lace is adjusted (which once adjusted need not be altered).

When taking off Corsets, to release belt from side studs, draw forward and outwards.

8

DIRECTIONS

First, spread the Corset out on the bed, then lay down on it; now fasten the busks in front, then take a belt in either hand and draw outward until the desired pressure is obtained; now fasten on side studs, and then buckle belt to front lappet; you may then stand up and adjust the waist lace as desired.

Or another way is to put the Corset on loosely while standing up, fasten the suspenders, then lay down and adjust as before, but you will find the former way the best.

If you have not tried this method of applying your Corsets you will always adopt it after having once experienced the added comfort and advantages obtained.

For stout ladies a very much smarter figure is obtained by applying the Corset in this way.

Figure 2
The Jenyns' Patent: promotional booklet c.1912
Leicestershire County Council Museums Service, Symington Collection

who patented this design was from Brisbane and she described herself as a 'Ladies Surgical Instrument Maker'. This corset was relatively expensive, retailing for 19 shillings and 6 pence and aimed at the fashionable market.[6] A skilled self-publicist, Mrs Jenyns assured women that wearing her corset would not injure health in spite of tight lacing and strapping. Visually, it seems clear to the modern viewer that a more restrictive and retraining garment could scarcely be imagined.

Both the dresses chosen for the exhibition from the pre-1914 period exhibit the prevalent exuberance encouraged by fashion, for both day and evening wear. As Oscar Wilde's character Lord Illingsworth declared in *A Woman of No Importance* in 1893 "Moderation is a fatal thing, Lady Hunstanton. Nothing succeeds like excess."[7]

Indeed, the dramatic dress labelled 'G Worth' shows not only complex construction and layering, but also allusions to masculine costume and 18th century revival styles as seen in the mock waistcoat fronts, the 'tailored tailcoat' and the sleeve ruffles. This type of historicism runs as a *leit motif* through the work of House of Worth in this period as shown in the surviving photographic archives at the V&A and the Museum of Costume, Bath.[8] Although the exact model has so far eluded discovery, there are a number of outfits with similar features. It requires considerable imagination for us now to imagine this highly elaborate and aristocratic visiting costume as practical daywear.

The other outfit from our collection is more typical of Edwardian evening wear, with a bottle green silk satin under-dress, entirely covered by a black net overdress, heavily embroidered with gold thread and black beading. It is unlabelled, and almost certainly the product of a high-end dressmaker.

Both the outfits also exemplify the use of labour-intensive construction, lavishly costly silks, contrasting colours and embroidered trim. The Gallery of Costume's collection currently includes 270 dresses dating from 1900 to 1914, some of them equally elaborate. It must be acknowledged, however, that in some aspects, the overloaded elaboration of dress in the high Edwardian period (1905-10) was already softening and simplifying in the immediate pre-1914 period, and thus cannot be laid solely at the door of war. However it was a process vastly intensified during the First World War as social life itself simplified and clothing – for women as much as for men – needed to be more functional and practical. It became essentially unpatriotic to maintain the intricacies of frequent changes of clothes or dressing for dinner, or to wear conspicuously expensive clothing.

If the expectations on many women magnified with the war effort, so, too, their opportunities expanded. With fewer men in the workforce, women were called upon to work in transport and in factories, and volunteered for auxiliary roles in the military services. Manchester has a number of these auxiliary uniforms, all of which show clear masculine influence through their tailoring and design, especially in the jackets. The Women's Royal Naval Service (WRNS) uniform that has been selected dates from 1918 and was worn by Sybil Aspinall who joined the WRNS in October 1918 and served for a year, finishing as a deputy principal.[9] This is another example of a costume collected by the Cunningtons where we have been able to discover details of the wearer, this time because her name was inscribed on an inner label. Other women's uniforms represented in the collection include a Women's Army Auxiliary Corps uniform from 1917, a Land Army uniform also from 1917 and a Red Cross Society uniform.

Post-war society sought to recover from trauma and dislocation. However, nearly a million British men had been killed and many young women were destined to remain single, propelling them to independence. Pre-war norms were only partially re-established as working women often refused to submit to previous restrictions, for instance, of live-in household service. In its various incarnations, the Female Suffrage Movement had fought a long campaign up until 1914. Female suffrage became law in 1918 for property owners over 30, encountering little of the weight of pre-war opposition.

After the war, opportunities for relatively 'genteel' work in telecommunications and retail, and in the teaching and nursing professions, grew for women throughout the 1920s. In leisure, women of means could participate in a range of sports or they could travel and holiday alone; they could go to fashionable bars and dance halls, where they, like men, could smoke cigarettes and drink cocktails. Young women, in particular, were encouraged by fashion magazines to wear make-up and to sport increasingly short hairstyles. Unsurprisingly, fashion also transformed.

By the middle 1920s, the boyish female silhouette had triumphed. Whether for day or evening events, dresses were cut in simple shapes without emphasis on the natural waist and deliberately masking the bust. Hemlines shortened throughout the early 1920s until they reached the knee in 1926. Decoration could be either bold, unfussy and 'art deco', or flat and painterly, using the tubular shape as a canvas. Such shapes visually represented a new freedom, liberation from the restrictions of Edwardian social restraint. They also heralded the arrival of a new mass consumerism: the simplicity of women's fashions made them far cheaper than the pre-War outfits and ensured that ready-made, 'off-the-peg' clothing was easily available.

Both the 1920s dresses in the exhibition have similar uncomplicated shaping contrasting dramatically with the pre-war fashion. The orange silk evening dress is fully beaded and a typical 'flapper' dance dress, decorated to be seen in movement. Its contemporary design incorporates stylised hieroglyphics and is inspired by the greatest historical discovery of the 1920s, the tomb of Tutankhamun in 1923.[10]

The day dress in boldly striped green/cream Macclesfield silk strikes the contemporary viewer as modern and unpretentious, eminently wearable today, suitable for a host of summer activities.[11] This dress belonged to Miss Finch-Dawson from Penrith, Cumbria and was first worn by her to attend the Hendon Air Show in 1927.

The 1928 corset also differs dramatically from its Edwardian counterpart. The lightly boned corselette incorporates elastic side panels to provide some support for a figure used to more considerable corsetry, whilst combining as a garment with *crepe de chine* cami-knickers. Far more underwear than armour, it suggests emancipation from the worst of Edwardian restrain and confinement in fashion. Although it is simplistic to suggest that women of the later 1920s had been freed from all fashionable fetters – after all, the required silhouette was gamine, boyish and slim, with flattened bust and narrow hips – even so, compared to the restrictions of the immediate post-war period, they had indeed secured a certain liberty.

Dr. Miles Lambert, Curator of Costume,
Manchester City Galleries

1   Jane Webb *The Colourful Life of Clothes: telling tales from the dress archives*, Introduction (manuscript copy: publication by Bloomsbury in 2018)
2   Collection Manchester City Galleries 1940.456
3   Collection Manchester City Galleries 1947.4254
4   Jane Webb op cit
5   'The Jenyns' Patent Reducing and Supporting Corset', c.1912: Symington Collection, D602
6   Catalogue notes by Christopher Page: Symington Collection
7   *The works of Oscar Wilde*, Galley Press, Leicester, 1987, Act 3, p. 449
8   House of Worth photographic archives: see Amy de la Haye & Valerie D Mendes: *The House of Worth*, V&A Publishing, 2014
9   Collection Manchester City Galleries 1947.2535
10 Collection Manchester City Galleries 1956.323
11 Collection Manchester City Galleries 1968.187

Afternoon dress 1907-9
Shot silk, plain silk and silk net
Label: G. Worth, Paris
Collection Manchester City Galleries 1947.4254

Gaston Worth (1856-1926) was one of the two sons of Charles Frederick Worth, an Englishman who set up his atelier in Paris and is celebrated as fashion's first couturier. Gaston carried on the running of House of Worth after their father's death in 1895. This striking dress shows not only complex construction and layering, but also multi-facetted allusions to masculine costume and to the 18th century revivalism in dress. This dress was owned by Mrs Claude Watney, who was the wife of a brewing heir – and an early motorcar enthusiast. Highly elaborate and aristocratic, this visiting costume requires a stretch of the imagination today to be seen as practical daywear.

Evening dress 1910-12
Silk satin and silk net with embroidery
Collection Manchester City Galleries 1940.456

This costume is typical of late Edwardian evening wear with short sleeves and elaborate decoration. Perhaps intended for an older woman, the usual bare neckline has been covered by a modesty infill in snowy white lace. The green satin under-dress is entirely covered by a black net overdress, lavishly embroidered with gold thread and black beads.

The decoration is characteristically art nouveau in inspiration, with a linear design running from the waist to the hem. Unlabelled, the dress was almost certainly produced by a high-end dressmaker.

Day dress 1927
Silk
Collection Manchester City Galleries 1968.187

By the middle 1920s the androgynous silhouette had triumphed in fashionable circles. Whether for daywear or evening wear, dresses were cut in simple shapes without emphasis on the natural waist and de-emphasising the bust. Hemlines shortened throughout the early 1920s until they reached the knee by 1926. This dress in green and cream stripes, in a variety of widths, conveys a modernity which would make it a prime candidate for the retro re-wearing market. Made of silk rather than the cheaper cotton, it presents as a smart summer ensemble and was acquired by its original owner for a visit to the Hendon Air Show in summer 1927.

Evening dress 1923-4
Silk crepe, fully beaded
Collection Manchester City Galleries 1956.323

Dresses in the 1920s present a strikingly less elaborate silhouette than pre-war costume. This evening dress is intensely colourful, with beading covering every inch of the fabric. A typical 'flapper' dance dress, it would have shimmered seductively in night-time lighting and in movement, perfect for evenings in the new dance halls. The simple tubular shape presents the body as a canvas for decoration, and the design imitates Ancient Egyptian hieroglyphs. Following the discovery of Tutankhamun's tomb in 1923 'Egyptomania' spread and influenced contemporary design tastes. Egyptian decorative and figurative motifs appeared widely on textiles and accessories, and the silhouettes of ancient dress were re-created in the 1920s.

Women's Royal Naval Service uniform 1918
Wool twill
Label: Simpson & Suter, Ordnance Row,
Portsmouth & Cork St, London
Collection Manchester City Galleries 1947.2535

The Women's Royal Naval Service (WRNS) was founded in 1917 and by the end of the First World War, had over 5,000 members. This uniform was worn by Sybil Aspinall, who joined the WRNS in October 1918 and served for a year, finishing as a Deputy Principal. The WRNS was disbanded in 1919, but then revived in 1939 on the outbreak of the Second World War. Other women's uniforms from the First World War represented in the collection (but not on display here) include a Women's Army Auxiliary Corps uniform, Land Army uniform and a Red Cross Society uniform.

Undergarments:

The fashions for women before and after the First World War required very different undergarments. The two examples here demonstrate how foundation garments engineered the fashionable silhouette to great extremes.

Jenyns' corset 1911
Cotton; strapping and lacing
Courtesy Leicestershire County Council Museum Services,
Symington Collection

This rather daunting and imposing corset was patented and manufactured in Australia in 1911. Mrs E R Jenyns, who patented the design, was from Brisbane and was an early assured self-publicist. The promotional leaflet for her corset survives, and provides instructions for its wearing, together with a range of dramatic promises for health and posture benefits. Of course, the true purpose was to mould the figure by compressing the waist and hips and pushing up the bust. This was a fairly expensive garment, costing 19 shillings and 6 pence and clearly for fashionable commerce.

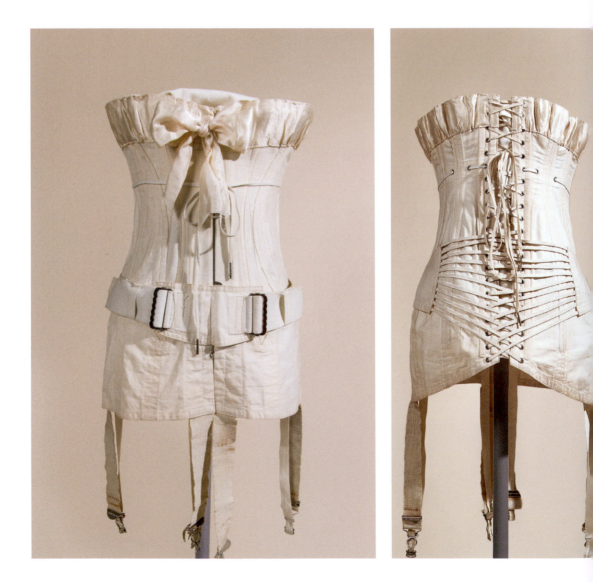

Corselette 1928
Figured rayon, *crepe de chine* and elastic
Courtesy Leicestershire County Council Museum Services,
Symington Collection

The appearance of this corselette exemplifies the dramatic transformation of underwear in the seventeen years since the Jenyns corset. Only lightly boned, it looks instead to the newer medium of elastic to 'persuade' the figure into shape. The corset has moved towards more feminine underwear, combining with *crepe de chine* cami-knickers and including four adjustable suspenders in decoratively frilled elastic. Although still moulding the figure, it suggests a certain move to modernity and freedom.

Re-dressing the Balance

I was invited by 14-18 NOW to create a project with Manchester Art Gallery which looked at the First World War and its impact on fashion. I was interested in how the roles of women changed and how this was then reflected in their dress. Whilst relishing the opportunity to include historic costume in the exhibition, I wanted the project to have a strong contemporary focus, with designers creating new pieces inspired by history. What I wanted to achieve was a mix of commissions of new ensembles by leading designers alongside emerging talent from fashion colleges, animated by fashion films.

Fashion & Freedom is first and foremost a celebration of women – their strength, creativity and resilience. Although the First World War had many negative outcomes for the United Kingdom, it fast-tracked women's rights as they took over traditional male roles during the war. *Fashion & Freedom* is a reflection on that time through the eyes of today's leading established and emerging female designers.

This is the first time such an eminent group of female designers have come together and created specially commissioned pieces inspired by the stories and experiences of working women 100 years ago. It shows how the silhouettes from a century ago are still the bedrock of our catwalks and high streets today and also that although great strides were made towards equality, there is still a long way to go.

Vivienne Westwood is the grande dame of British fashion as well as its most anti-establishment figure. Over the last four decades her collections have portrayed a strong female identity and her boiler suit with a disco twist perfectly brings together her spirit of glamour and rebellion.

Roksanda Ilincic is an award-winning designer known for her signature bold block colours and effortlessly modern silhouette. Her piece takes inspiration from the women who worked in the munitions factories during the First World War. Often working without protection, they suffered TNT poisoning which turned their skin yellow. Ilincic's piece, in vibrant canary yellow, shines a light on the bravery and commitment of those women.

Holly Fulton is a leading womenswear and accessories designer, known for her meticulous approach to pattern and striking graphic motifs. She has also explored the stories of the munitionettes. Fulton has turned the patterns formed by the shells in the factories into a decorative motif that has been applied to silk organza, evoking the imagery witnessed by the women in the factories.

Emilia Wickstead worked in leading international fashion houses before establishing her own successful brand. Known for her modern take on classic couture, her work combines exquisite craftsmanship with graceful feminine silhouettes. Wickstead was inspired by the Dazzle Ships' experimental graphic camouflage used extensively in the First World War.

Jackie JS Lee opened London Fashion Week in February 2016. A specialist pattern cutter, she has built an influential brand known for sharp, clean and feminine silhouettes. She has chosen work-wear as her focus, looking to men's tailoring and the trouser, using a colour palette drawn from the trenches.

Sadie Williams is a name to watch. Her work is futuristic, combining metallic textiles with playful colours and patterns. Williams has chosen to celebrate the women on the front line, the Voluntary Aid Detachments or VAD's who worked for the Red Cross, an 'angelic homage' to those brave and resilient superwomen.

As well as the designer commissions, I was keen to include film to bring physical movement, strength and energy to the exhibition. I am delighted that Nick Knight's SHOWstudio, a platform for today's most influential fashion filmmakers, are contributing to the project. Over the last 15 years, SHOWstudio have been truly ground breaking in establishing fashion film as a new genre.

As well as fashion films, I also wanted a more intimate narrative short to bring to life the personal story of a young woman going to work for the first time. It's easy to take this for granted today in the UK, but a century ago the ability to join the workforce and undertake new roles was faced by a huge number of young women. *First* by filmmaker Luke Snellin, and with costumes by Manchester's own Private White V.C., takes us back to this extraordinary moment of change.

Fashion & Freedom is looking to the past but is focused firmly on the future. In keeping with this, I wanted to give an opportunity to the next generation of talented creatives. I invited young designers from the UK's fashion colleges to respond to the themes of either *Restriction* or *Release*. *Restriction* representing pre-war (a world of corsets, heavy long skirts and no voting rights) and *Release* representing post-war (emancipation, the invention of the bra and free flowing silhouette). The students have created exceptional contemporary responses to these themes.

I am hugely grateful to all the designers, filmmakers, students, photographers and stylists for their brilliance and creativity.

Darrell Vydelingum, Creative Director, *Fashion & Freedom*

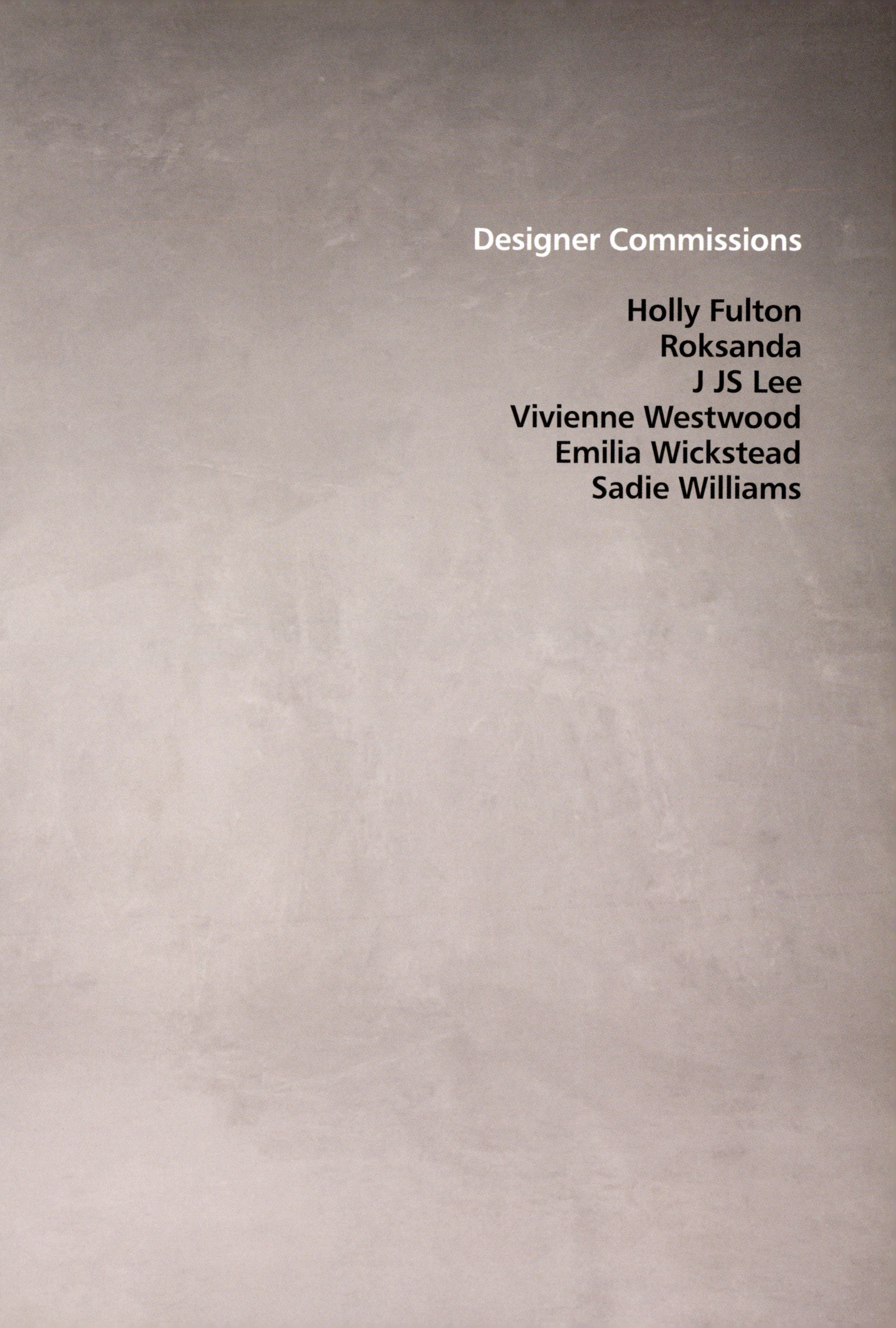

Designer Commissions

Holly Fulton
Roksanda
J JS Lee
Vivienne Westwood
Emilia Wickstead
Sadie Williams

Holly Fulton

"I was fascinated by the munitionettes, or canary girls…I thought about the emancipation women were working towards, but also how vanity must have suffered because handling TNT turned their skin yellow and their hair green."

Holly Fulton is a womenswear and accessories designer living and working in East London. Born in Scotland, she studied in Edinburgh before going on to do a Masters at the Royal College of Art. She established her label in 2009 and won numerous industry prizes for her work, which is characterised by graphic embellishment and couples digitally manipulated print with various textile fabrications.

Holly Fulton's design was inspired by her research on the experience of the female munitions workers during and after the First World War. After learning that there was a munitions factory near the Hackney Marshes, where she currently lives, Fulton reflected upon the hazardous environment of the factories, and the social transitions occurring as women were employed in weapons manufacture. Fulton consulted photographs of the factories and incorporates elements from her research in the final design.

"The patterns formed by the mounds of shells in the factories were mesmeric. I wanted my design to incorporate elements from the workers' dress and also have a graphic root in these patterns."

The colour palette of yellow and black refers to the skin discolouration suffered by the workers and also the growing fashionability of black clothing after the First World War. The wool zip-neck jumper alludes to knitted undergarments, with a nod towards the increased functionality of women's everyday dress post-war. The merino wool used for the coat and trousers references the British textile and garment manufacturing trades. The ensemble is accessorised with earrings made of industrial elements and gloves based on the gauntlets worn by the factory workers.

Holly Fulton 2016
Dress: Satinised organza with digital embroidery, laser-cut appliqués and hand applied details
Jumper: Merino wool; courtesy John Smedley
Coat: Cashmere with silk embroidery
Gloves: Leather; courtesy Dents
Shoes: Christian Laboutin for Holly Fulton

Roksanda

"As a designer I have always been fascinated with freedom and communication and what fashion brings to our lives. Therefore *Fashion & Freedom* was something that really attracted my attention. It gave me a deeper knowledge of what women went through to gain their independence, something which is often taken for granted in our time. I wanted to embody the spirit of those brave women who played such an instrumental role in the changes to women's status during the First World War."

After studying architecture and applied arts in her native Belgrade, Roksanda Ilincic came to London where she earned her masters degree in Womenswear at Central Saint Martins. She has been showing her collections at London Fashion Week since 2005. Ilincic's signature silhouettes and her bold use of colour make for collections with an unmistakably modern approach to luxury fashion.

Her piece for *Fashion & Freedom* was inspired by the plight and pride of the female munitions workers during the First World War, who suffered chemical poisoning which discoloured the skin.

"For my colour palette I found particular inspiration in the work of the canary girls, incredible women whose skin turned yellow as a result of working closely with toxic chemicals. For my shape, I was inspired by learning of the gradual acceptance for women to wear trousers at work because they were more practical. This was a revolution in itself and I wanted the look to reflect this huge change in fashion. Strong women who embrace femininity are always a source of inspiration in my collections. I love the duality of that spirit."

Roksanda 2016
Dress: Cotton/silk dupion blend, with silk organza and cotton trim
Trousers: Open-weave silk gazar
Shoes: Nicholas Kirkwood for Roksanda

J JS Lee

"We owe a huge amount of respect to the women who fought for their rights during the First World War period. As women today we have them to thank for many of the opportunities we have. For me, this project was a very different way of working and approach to design. Usually I am inspired by my own personal experiences but here I had to try and understand the women of this time – it was a very emotional journey. I felt an enormous sense of responsibility to produce an ensemble that helps tell their story and celebrate these brave women who changed our futures."

Born in Seoul, Korea, Jackie Lee established her eponymous label J JS Lee after studying at Central Saint Martins. Her MA collection received international critical acclaim and was honoured with the Harrod's Award in 2010. Her collections are built around her vision of the modern woman who dresses in sharp silhouettes, with androgynous tailoring but in a unique feminine way.

For *Fashion & Freedom* Lee was inspired by wartime aesthetics and practices – uniforms, recycling of textiles, restricted colour palettes and the transition towards women wearing trousers. She references the change in the silhouette from long skirts to trousers in her design which incorporates leg-warmers as an underlayer to knee-length skirts.

Lee's pieces for *Fashion & Freedom* were also inspired by the end of the wartime period:

"I looked at Vogue covers from 1918 and noticed how they evoked the feeling of the time – a sense of freedom. The war had just finished and British and French flags were featured and celebrated. It was a time for women to celebrate and embrace their new found freedoms whilst fighting to retain this new independence and their place within society."

J JS Lee 2016
Wool crepe, wool tweed
Shoes: Wool crepe and leather

Vivienne Westwood

"Our rotten financial system creates poverty for the many, riches for the few.

We have a war economy.

Almost everyone supported the First World War and the press must take responsibility for the nationalistic propaganda that helped to create this terrible ethos.

We still have the same system in place – a war economy.

We now know that this system – and the arms trade – helps create climate change – we are facing mass extinction.

Fight the system and replace it with a green economy."

Vivienne Westwood began designing in 1971 along with her then partner Malcolm McLaren. They used their shop at 430 Kings Road, London, to showcase their ideas and designs, changing not only the name of the shop but also the décor. In 1976, Westwood and McLaren defined the street culture of punk with *Seditionaries*.

In 1981 Westwood showed her first catwalk presentation at Olympia in London. She turned to traditional Savile Row tailoring techniques, using British fabrics and 17th and 18th century art for inspiration.

In 1989 she met Andreas Kronthaler, who would later become her husband and design partner, as well as Creative Director of the brand. In 2006, her contribution to British Fashion was officially recognised when she was appointed Dame of the British Empire by Her Majesty, Queen Elizabeth II.

With a design career spanning four decades, Vivienne Westwood is now revered as one of the most influential fashion designers and activists in the world today. Westwood continues to capture the imagination, and raise awareness of environmental and human rights issues.

Vivienne Westwood
Gold Label Autumn-Winter 2006/07 *Innocent*
Runway show look #39, re-made 2016
Jumpsuit: Printed iridescent sequin on silk
Cardigan: Wool
Shoes: Clomper Slave Sandals in brown croc embossed leather

Emilia Wickstead

British-based and New Zealand born, Emilia Wickstead spent her formative years in Milan and graduated from Central Saint Martins in 2007. She worked at Armani, Proenza Schouler, Narciso Rodriguez and Vogue in New York and Milan, before returning to London to establish her own label in 2008, showing at London Fashion Week since 2012.

Emilia Wickstead's piece for *Fashion & Freedom* was informed by her research into women's societal and "political evolution" during and after the First World War and examination of dazzle camouflage, used on navy vessels during the war. Her piece reflects her aim to show the dual nature of the situation for women after the war.

"When I researched the dazzle ships of the First World War, I was drawn to their appearance and design – I found there was something modern and fresh in the way lines and patterns were used and this was a great starting point for my design. Once I looked into dazzle ships further I found that they were not used purely for camouflage; their main purpose was not to conceal but to confuse – this to me represents the changing attitudes to, and perceptions of, women after the war as society and its restrictions were shifting.

Each ship was unique and this was such a unique time for women; I am so inspired by their ability to secure comfort and happiness whilst they are exploring their identity.

Emilia Wickstead 2016
Wool
Shoes: Charlotte Olympia for Emilia Wickstead

I wanted to show both elements of the post-war fashion culture – although women adapted hugely after the war, there was still a certain degree of conservatism in dress which I reference in the hem line and neck of the dress. The holes in the middle represent the breaking of molds – women having become freer to do and wear what they wanted. They also suggest the lifebuoys thrown out to sea during the war. I think here is something quite romantic about the notion of the saviour and the sentiments of the men returning from the war and back to their loved ones.

For me this project was really about experimenting with the way women dress and pushing boundaries, in an almost conservative way. It's a bit of an oxymoron – which made it so important to get the aesthetic of the dress just right."

Sadie Williams

"I took inspiration from the colours and clean shapes of Red Cross uniforms from the First World War. Yet I wanted to steer away from practicality and instead create an angelic glistening gown as homage to these super women, complete with the Red Cross symbol proudly adorning the chest, like a super-hero emblem."

Sadie Williams is a fashion and textile designer, born and based in London. She studied on the Central Saint Martins MA Fashion course and her work is characterised by playful juxtapositions of material, colour, texture and form.

After graduating, she went on to become one of Selfridges *Bright Young Things* in 2013, showcasing a range of embossed mini-dresses and lurex-print sweatshirts. A selection of her MA collection dresses were put on display in a window at Selfridges, Oxford Street, London. The dresses were made from a new shimmering textile Williams innovated.

For *Fashion & Freedom* Williams has created a new work from this textile as an homage to women working for the Red Cross as Voluntary Aid Detachments (VADs) during the First World War.

"I found it very moving to think of all these women signing up to protect sick and wounded victims of war, putting on their nursing uniforms and proudly bearing the Red Cross emblem on their chests. I've always been very drawn to bold print arrangements and graphic motifs and the symbol of the Red Cross is something I find very inspirational for many reasons. It's incredibly visually impactful whilst signifying both protection and neutrality."

Sadie Williams 2016
Polyester lurex bonded to cotton track-suiting

Restriction / Release

Leeds College of Art
London College of Fashion
Manchester School of Art
University of Salford
University of Westminster

Restriction / Release is a project showcasing the next generation of fashion talent from five universities who responded to the social and sartorial changes brought about by the First World War. The emerging creatives are students from Leeds College of Art, London College of Fashion, Manchester School of Art, the University of Salford and the University of Westminster and were selected from numerous submissions. They have responded to either the theme of pre-war *Restriction* or post-war *Release*, and two students from London College of Fashion were invited to respond to both. Two teams of students from Leeds College of Art interpreted their research by producing fashion photographs that reflect the stories and themes of the project.

Cherry Ng

"*Stride* reflects the changes after the war. Although women had gained much, unfair treatment was still restricting them. This is the reason I kept elastic bands in the design, which shows that they are not locked but still controlled."

The inspiration for both of these designs came from the dazzle patrol ships during the First World War and the experience and uniforms of women factory workers. The designer explored not only the changes the war brought about socially, but also in the visual arts. To her, dazzle ships are an emblem of art and of war: the pattern is a work of art but with a military function. Ng echoed the effect and appearance of dazzle camouflage through the use of pleats which create visual confusion. She used the technique on both garments, in different ways as reflections on conservatism in the pre and post-war periods.

Cherry Ng
BA Hons Fashion Design Technology Womenswear, London College of Fashion

Restriction: Locked 2016
Silk, Latex-coated cotton, PVC, leather, metal

Release: Stride 2016
Silk, leather, PVC, metal

Xenia Telunts

"Early aviatrix Amy Johnson became my primary inspiration. Her courage and devotion led her to achievements which gave faith to many women – that they too would be able to reach their goals."

The inspiration for Xenia Telunts' *Restriction* piece came from researching the poor conditions of Victorian workhouses and asylums, where some women were consigned who suffered mental distress due to the effects of the First World War. Telunts' work suggests a straight-jacket, as a reference to women's restricted position in society and the struggle to support their families financially. She chose to make the dress in white to symbolise innocence and the hope for a brighter future, with black banding as a symbol of repression.

The *Release* piece *Pilot* references early aviation and powerful, working women during and after the war. It has a masculine silhouette and was inspired in particular by one luminary woman, early aviatrix, Amy Johnson. A child during the First World War, she was later celebrated for being the first female pilot to fly from England to Australia in 1930 and she served in the Air Transport Auxiliary during the Second World War.

Xenia Telunts
BA Hons Fashion Design Technology Womenswear, London College of Fashion

Restriction: Pauper 2016 (left)
Poplin, polycotton binding, elastic

Release: Pauper 2016 (right)
Poplin, polycotton binding, elastic

Beth Blears, Beth Cowling, Ben Lewis

"Photographing in a studio environment allowed us to create a set and develop a modern interpretation of *Restriction*. Our choice of camera angles created a strong female identity as a contrast to repression."

Blears, Cowling and Lewis were informed by research into Edwardian dress silhouettes, foundation garments and social codes for fashion during the First World War. The full length black gown of heavy velvet emphasises *Restriction*, inactivity and confinement. Classic horror films and imagery of early deep-sea diving helmets inspired the design of the neckpiece – a symbol of the lack of female voices in society and politics prior to women's suffrage.

Beth Blears: Creative direction and styling
Beth Cowling: Creative direction and styling
Ben Lewis: Creative direction and garment design
BA Hons Fashion Concepts and Communications,
Leeds College of Art

Restriction 2016
Photography: Karl Spencer
Model: Nicole Thompson
Corset courtesy of OrchidCorset.com

Jessica Bachmann

"I focused on the concept of *Restriction* and the experience of the Suffragettes…while referencing the contemporary artist Harald Nägeli and his abstract studies of women."

Jessica Bachmann's approach to design is influenced by her background in art history and conservation. For her response to *Restriction / Release* she was particularly inspired by the work of Picasso and Harald Nägeli and explored how the human body can be strung into unusual shapes by a garment. School uniforms during the First World War and the strictures of the education system were also conceptual and design inspirations.

Taking Picasso's work *The Acrobat* 1930 as a template, Bachmann has translated it into a garment pattern that wraps around the body. It turns and twists, evoking the theme of *Restriction* and women's struggle to redefine their gender roles during the First World War.

Jessica Bachmann
BA Hons Fashion Design, Manchester School of Art

Passing The Dress-Code (In Memory of the Suffragettes)
2016
Cotton, leather, synthetic materials

Morgane Davies

"I researched all sorts of military backpack shapes and was fascinated by the amount of detail that could be found on them, from stitching to pocket bags, eyelets, straps and strings."

Morgane Davies' piece takes inspiration from a First World War's soldier's kit, which was a mobile but cumbersome survival tool. Associating this image with that of street vendors overburdened with heavy loads, she researched ways of designing a piece that would reference the experience of the soldier.

The final work resulted from an obsessive study of the functional details on Army-issue backpacks. The effect is of something that appears overloaded but offers a poetic fashion interpretation of the notion of soldiers carrying their whole lives on their back.

Morgane Davies
BA Hons Fashion Design, University of Westminster

Carrying 2015
Cotton canvas, leather, metal

Revekka Georgiadou

"I wanted to evoke the munitionettes' feelings of embarrassment…designing garments that restrict the body from moving freely but also creating an exaggerated silhouette, echoing the environment of the factories and shapes of the bullet shells."

In her research, Georgiadou consulted testimonials from the women who worked in munitions factories and her design is a tribute to their story. The women workers were nicknamed munitionettes, but also canaries because the chemical exposure they suffered while preparing bullet shells discoloured the skin, turning their hands yellow. The choice of colours, materials and silhouette in this design are all symbolic tributes to the female war workers.

Revekka Georgiadou
BA Hons Fashion Design, University of Salford

The Caged Canary 2016
Silk crepe, aluminium

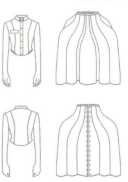

OUTFIT 5

Outfit five includes a tailored shirt that extends to the hands, where is dip-dyed with canary yellow latex. The shirt has a stand-up neck collar and and identification tag patch. The bottom part consists a full skirt with round panelled box pleats that are manipulated into pockets, and a ribbon belt to hold the waist tightly and exaggerate the shape of the shirt.

Fastenings: Shirt's button stand and bright, canary yellow, heavy-duty metal zip at the back of the skirt.

Accessories: Ribbon belt.

William R. Howell-Jackson

"The cut of the tight bodice explodes upwards into two bird-like bustle sleeves that congregate in the centre back as an offering – a symbol of remembrance."

William Howell-Jackson drew on his deep interest in fashion history and knowledge of couture construction in response to the themes of *Restriction / Release*. For *Christabel* he was inspired by Edwardian images of female spectators at Ascot before the start of the First World War. He also researched and employed a technique developed by 20th century fashion designer Charles James to create volume in dresses, using quilted layers of horsehair, cotton organza and silk.

Christabel incorporates a pair of vintage culottes sourced at London's second-hand clothing market on Portobello Road. Howell-Jackson reworked them so the waist became the bodice whilst retaining the volume of the legs which become two explosive sleeves. The design and silhouette are the result of the designer's research into historic dressmaking techniques and his reflection upon the Suffragette movement.

William R. Howell-Jackson
BA Hons Fashion Design, University of Westminster

Christabel 2015
Cotton, silk

Toni Martin

"There is always flesh beneath the dress!"

In her design, Toni Martin references the extreme corsetry of the pre-First World War period, in sharp contrast to how the pendulum of fashion would swing towards liberation of the body after the war. The dress reform movement of the early 1900s sought to free the female body from constrictive clothing. Corsets, and other restrictive clothing, caused women health problems and were unsuitable for modern life and work. Martin's piece sits between fashion and sculpture and addresses social and cultural issues, while offering a surreal vision of a controversial fashion item.

Toni Martin
BA Hons Fashion Design, University of Salford

Breathe In 2016
Wood, wool

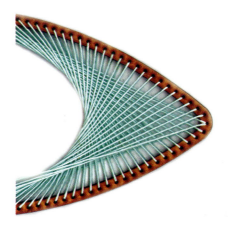

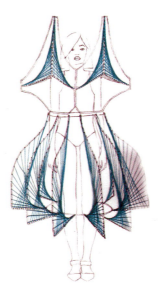

Elizabeth Thomas

"I have long been interested in how women were subjugated by the fashions of their time… but after doing some research into late Victorian dress, I noticed that the expensive fabrics, length of dresses and the ornamentation of sleeves could be as restrictive as the sculpting underwear beneath."

Elizabeth Thomas explored the notion that women were "an excellent ornament to man"[1] and how this was exemplified by excessive decoration in Victorian and Edwardian fashion. Thomas emphasises the role of ornament in creating restrictions on the female body. She incorporates frills and flounces into her design and exaggerates the length of the dress and height of the collar to suggest imprisonment within fashion and the stifling of women's voices. Although the silhouette suggests *Restriction*, she wanted there to be a certain frothiness to the design, inspired by James Tissot's painting *Hush!* 1875 in Manchester City Galleries collection.

---

1   Cornelius A. Lapide *Omnes divi pauli Epistolas Commentaria* 1638

Elizabeth Thomas
BA Hons Fashion Design, Manchester School of Art

An Excellent Ornament of Man 2016
Lace, silk, taffeta, tulle

James Tissot *Hush!* 1875 (detail)
Collection Manchester City Galleries

Olivia Johnson, Alice Lambert Hallam, Gina Mason

"We chose our location to reflect women's struggle for equality – towards having more career and educational opportunities. For us the library represented a woman's right to a better education."

This photo essay traces the changing silhouette of women's fashion during and after the First World War. The progression shows the cumbersome crinoline being stripped away, creating a new silhouette. This demonstrates how women's clothing became more practical as they took on physically challenging jobs during the war. The poses of the model also evolve from tenseness and control to more relaxed shapes, symbolising social freedoms.

Olivia Johnson
Alice Lambert Hallam
Gina Mason
BA Hons Fashion Concepts and Communications,
Leeds College of Art

Release 2016
Photography: Ben Renshaw
Photography Assistant: Jenny Briggs
Model: Matilda Wilson
Hair and Make-Up: Emily Richardson

Joana Almagro Bustalino

"The inspiration behind my design is Emmeline Pankhurst and the Suffragettes – a tribute to women working together to gain the right to vote."

Inspired by the Suffragette slogan *'Women Voters: Conquer Freedom'*, this design expresses the notion of *Release* through women attaining the right to vote. It adapts the colour scheme associated with the Suffragettes and alludes to the changes in the fashionable silhouette in the periods before and after the First World War. Freedom is further symbolised by the many panels of pleats around the skirt with a zip suggesting the possibility of shortened hemlines.

Joana Almagro Bustalino
BA Hons Fashion Design, Manchester School of Art

Women Voters: Conquer Freedom 2016
Organza, silk dupion (embroidered and beaded)

Sarah Curtis

"I began my research by visiting my local training grounds and speaking to young female footballers today to start to understand all aspects of the game."

The inspiration for this piece came from the extraordinary story of how women played football to stay fit while undertaking strenuous jobs in munitions factories during the First World War. Playing during their lunch hour, the munitionettes formed their own teams and competed, socialising and keeping their spirits high. Record-breaking player Lily Parr, who scored over 1000 goals, served as the muse for Curtis' design. The pioneering, strong and active women of Parr's team *Dick Kerr and the Ladies*, inspired the use of fabrics and shapes that transform with movement, incorporating the symbols, colours and textures of conventional football kits.

Sarah Curtis
BA Hons Fashion Design, University of Salford

Outlaws 2016
Cotton, leather, neoprene, powermesh

FRONT   BACK

Karin Human

"During a time when woman were often seen but not heard, the Suffragettes stood up for themselves using a martial art relying solely on gravity...."

In designing this ensemble, Karin Human took her inspiration from a group of Suffragettes who trained in martial arts. Their aim was to serve and protect their leader Emmeline Pankhurst during marches and protests, by being able to quickly assemble into formation, then seamlessly disappear into the crowd. The textile design re-interprets the Suffragettes' colours of green and purple and the silhouette references both East Asian dress and the dress reform styles associated with the women's movement in the late 19th and early 20th centuries.

Karin Human
BA Hons Fashion Design, University of Salford

The Pattern of Protection 2016
Cotton, leather, nylon

Rebecca Lawton

"My colour palette was inspired by the stockings and tights of the post-First World War period. I found it interesting that women did not always wear just ordinary nude or black but also pastel coloured stockings…"

Rebecca Lawton's work took its inspiration from the idea of exposure in contrast to the bodily taboos that have historically governed women's dress and behaviour. After reading a magazine article, written just after the First World War, that encouraged women to roll their stockings down and reveal their knees, Lawton reflected on changing attitudes towards body exposure in female fashion. Inspired by the daring women who embraced the rolled stocking and even, on occasion, decorated their knees, she used embroidery rings to frame the formerly hidden body parts – referencing both female rebellion and the domestic practice of embroidery.

Rebecca Lawton
BA Hons Fashion Design, University of Salford

Roll'em Girls! 2016
Cotton sateen, nylon

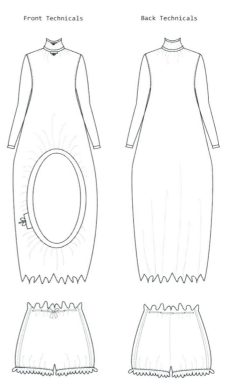

Front Technicals   Back Technicals

Wheiman Leong

"The net skirt incorporates faded flowers in white, brown and yellow – trying to liberate themselves from the pleats, striving for freedom."

Pendulum takes its inspirations from the traditional trench coat, a classic in fashion today, with roots in the First World War military standard issue. The design investigates notions of *Restriction* and *Release* simultaneously, through the pleating, draping and choice of hardware details. The design exposes the shoulder and arm to represent the liberation of women through voting rights. *Pendulum* also draws inspiration from German artist Anselm Kiefer whose work explores themes of war and its aftermath. *Pendulum* was directly inspired by his sculpture *Sprache der Vögel (Language of the Birds)* 1989 that portrays a stack of books with wide-open wings that are reminiscent of imperfect pleats.

Wheiman Leong
BA Hons Fashion Design, University of Westminster

Pendulum 2015
Nylon, polyester

Charlotte Malyon

"To create the many intricate gathers on the jacket I used materials such as dyed curtain tape and for the backpack, I used elastic to create the creasing… for each gather a piece of curtain tape was pulled at varied lengths until it produced the final silhouette."

Charlotte Malyon
BA Hons Fashion Design, University of Westminster

Parachute 2015
Nylon, polyester

Charlotte Malyon's piece draws inspiration from images of parachutes and skydiving, contrasting the release of a parachute with the restriction of its harness around the body. The large swathes of fabric left on the ground after landing from a jump also inspired her design.

The materials and mechanisms of the parachute have been incorporated into the design, based on Malyon's studies of an original parachute pattern and the MA1 flight jacket. The silhouette and volume have been achieved through the use of innovative pattern cutting techniques in tandem with draping on the dressmaker's stand.

Rebecca Webster

"In order to capture the sense of release following the First World War, I reflected on emptiness and the mixed emotions women were facing as they were forced to relinquish their newfound roles and responsibilities."

Rebecca Webster's piece takes Emelia Earhart, a pioneering aviator of the post-war period, as its muse. Earhart was described by the designer as an "adrenaline junkie", grasping opportunities to see the world through life-risking flight. Inspired by the excitement of floating and free falling in parachute jumps, Webster explored the drape and structure of their canopies and fastenings. A chance encounter with a tent trapped in a tree led Webster to experiment with airflow through fabrics. Her piece retains the delicacy and softness from her initial research imagery whilst also being inspired by engineering and aircraft design.

Rebecca Webster
BA Hons Fashion Design, Manchester School of Art

Flight 2016
Chiffon, organza

Film Commissions

**Luke Snellin *first*
SHOWstudio**

Fashion & Freedom includes a series of specially commissioned films. These works, collaborations amongst visionary directors and designers, provide contemporary reflections upon the social and cultural changes brought about by the First World War and are reflective of how historical events continue to inspire cutting-edge creative production.

Luke Snellin *first*

For *Fashion & Freedom* filmmaker Luke Snellin has written and directed a short narrative film entitled *first* which re-imagines a young woman's first day of work as a bus conductor during the First World War. The film stars Sai Bennett and features re-styled women's civic uniforms designed by Manchester fashion label Private White V.C.

Film credits:
Produced and edited by Luke Snellin
Co-Producers: Max Milner and Matthew Gallagher
Executive Producer: Darrell Vydelingum
Clothes: Private White V.C.
Costume Designer: Nick Ashley
Costume Supervisor: Lily Ashley
Costume Assistant: Beatrice Vermeir
Director of Photography: Carl Burke
Production Designer: Beck Rainford
Art Director: Freya Closs
Hair and Make up Designer: Alyn Waterman
Original Music: Jeremy Warmsley

Cast:
Sai Bennett
Marion Bailey
Dino Fetscher
Rebekah Staton
Sarah Sweeney
Dominique Moore
Roy North
Elizabeth Sankey
Matthew Stathers
Will Chitty

With thanks to: The London Bus Museum,
One Stop Films and Lee Lighting.

"The inspiration for the idea came from talking about the changes to women's fashion during the First World War. Women were given new responsibilities and pushed further towards equality as a result. The clothing reflected this, it became more officious and the cut and shapes began to shift towards more powerful and authoritative silhouettes.

So initially the concept came from the clothing but then thinking emotionally about a narrative, I started to consider what it must be like to face a first day at work when you are thought of as inferior or inadequate to do that job. There is a nervousness, an anxiety and drama – and yet pride and excitement at the opportunity to prove to people that you are capable.

I also liked the idea of a young woman's life changing over the course of her first day at work; for her individual story to be shadowing the changes in women's rights that were jump-started during the period. I wanted it to be a love story too and felt it just as important to tell the story of her beginning to fall in love as she starts her working life. The balance of these things was key to the tone of the film and to portraying her as a three-dimensional woman.

My idea was also to be slightly rebellious and try some things to distinguish the style from traditional period films. I wanted to combine loyalty to the period with subtle, more modern progressive details like a contemporary score, typography and other aesthetic details such as casting choices and the props and costumes."

About Private White V.C.

The fashion label Private White V.C. pays homage to its namesake, the First World War hero, Private Jack White. The clothing line has a subtle nod to Jack's military legacy, with many items based on classic wartime pieces, updated with added functionality and detail for the modern man.

All clothing is constructed by hand in the Private White V.C. factory in Manchester, where garments are designed and developed using the finest regionally sourced fabrics, trims and materials.

For *Fashion & Freedom*, Private White V.C. have designed and crafted the uniforms worn by the female workforce in *first*. The wool dresses are a contemporary take on the civic uniforms of the First World War, and were worn with period accessories to complete the look.

"My vision came full circle with Nick Ashley and Private White V.C. executing a modern, minimalist approach to the clothes which I think neatly underscores the connection between the two periods, one hundred years apart."

Luke Snellin

SIGNALLER

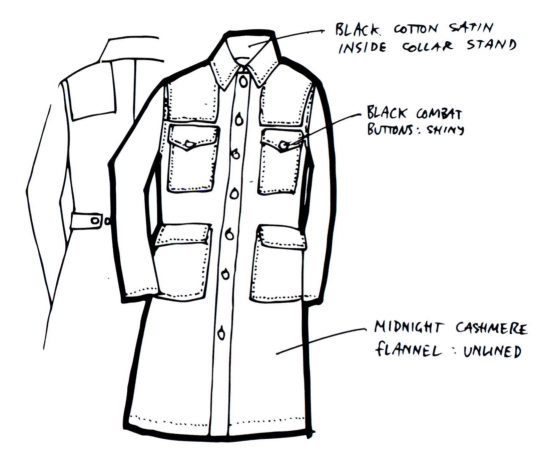

BLACK COTTON SATIN
INSIDE COLLAR STAND

BLACK COMBAT
BUTTONS: SHINY

MIDNIGHT CASHMERE
FLANNEL: UNLINED

* SILK STOCKINGS : BLACK
* BLACK COURT SHOES

SHOWstudio Film Commissions

SHOWstudio is the home of fashion film and has championed the medium since the site's inception in 2000. SHOWstudio also serves as an educational resource to young people, students and those interested in fashion – offering critical and considered series of films around historical fashion, current movements and the future of the industry.

"*Fashion & Freedom* is a very natural fit. When working out our plans, we chose to continue our commitment both to fashion film and, more widely, to supporting emerging talent, so selected from our wide range of brilliant contributors key creatives who are making waves in their respective fields."

Charlotte Knight, Executive Producer, SHOWstudio

'Untitled'

While many know Gareth Pugh for his interest in club culture and performance, he is respected throughout the industry as a master cutter and tailor, with a skill for precise fits and razor sharp lines and shoulders. Military wear, therefore, is the perfect avenue for him to explore when considering historical costume. Filmmaker George Harvey, who is known for his clean black and white aesthetic, has a similarly sharp, considered focus and so makes the perfect partner.

Director: George Harvey

Fashion Designer: Gareth Pugh

Fashion Historian:
Shonagh Marshall

Production: Stink Studios

With special thanks to
Carson McColl & Aine Geoghegan

These Women

Rising London talent Craig Green is known for combining humble fabrics such as calico and traditional, masculine silhouettes with cerebral concepts and emotions. His work is quiet and unassuming, yet moving and rousing. Workwear is a constant obsession in all his collections. He partners with Marie Schuller, a filmmaker known for her diverse focus and bold subject matters.

Director: Marie Schuller
Workwear Looks by Craig Green
Models: Ia at Models1, Gaby at Next and Xu at Storm
Stylist: Anna Pesonen
Choreographer: Del Mak
Director of Photography: Franklin Dow
Hair: Sofia Sjoo
Make Up: Yin Lee
Focus Puller: Will Hadley
Gaffer: Naomi Hancock
Camera and Lighting: SLV
Soundtrack: Kiat
Runner: Egle Andriuskeviciute

Edith
Starring Guinevere Van Seenus

To explore the fall of the corset, SHOWstudio commissioned Rei Nadal, a young Spanish filmmaker and artist who regularly explores themes of femininity, rights of passage and role-play within her work. Fashion designer Phoebe English was tasked with creating the garment – she was selected partly because of her focus on adorning and accentuating the body through laboured construction forms and handwork techniques. Stylist Ellie Grace Cumming, a regular collaborator of both Nadal and English, also lends her eye.

Director: Rei Nadal
Corset Designer: Phoebe English
Stylist: Ellie Grace Cumming
Director of Photography: Britt Lloyd

Produced by PRETTYBIRD
for SHOWstudio and
Manchester Art Gallery

Executive Producer: Juliette Larthe
Producer: Hannah Bellil

Make-up Artist: Laura Dominique
Hair Stylist: Cyndia Harvey
Set Design: Simon Costin
Manicurist: Mike Pocock

Handlers: Philip Ellis, Bradley Sharpe,
Harris Reed and Pablo Rousson

Phoebe English Design Assistant:
Megan Sharkey
Stylist Assistant: Ben Schofield
Make-up Assistant: Yae Pascoe
Hair Assistant: Jennifer Lil Buckley
Art Department Assistant:
Meriel Hunt
Handlers Casting: Philip Ellis

Production Coordinator:
Laura Thomas-Smith
Production Assistant: Ella Knight
1st Assistant Director: Bryony James

Focus Puller: Sean McDerrmot
Gaffer: Yan Murawski
Electrician: Hamza Twomey

Offline Editor: Raquel Couceiro for
SHOWstudio
Colourist: Houmam Abdallah at
Electric Theatre Collective

Special thanks to Nick Knight, Charlotte Knight, all at SHOWstudio, Myriam Obadiah at Elite Paris, Paula Jenna at Streeters, Angela Alberti at CLM, Direct Photographic, Pixi Pixel, RiDa Studios, Jess Hallett Casting, Ali Nejad and Daniel Fletcher.

SHOWstudio were kindly hosted by The London EDITION.

Guinevere wears:
Corset custom made for SHOWstudio by Phoebe English, bra worn underneath by Phoebe English, tights by Tabio, socks from the National Theatre Costume Hire.

Philip, Harris, Pedro and Bradley wear:
All black clothing Phoebe English, all socks from Glenmuir at SocksShop.co.uk, all boots from Costume Studio. All khaki clothing from The Vintage Showroom.

Afterword

The role fashion has played in our social and political history is often forgotten, and the First World War is no exception. Women went to work in factories and took on many other roles previously regarded as suitable only for men. Fashion also played a role in this story, which is why it is so exciting to see today's leading female designers revisit this significant moment through their own contemporary lens.

Fashion & Freedom is an unprecedented project, bringing together for the very first time our most influential female designers to create bespoke pieces inspired by an important moment in our history.

I am delighted to see our leading designers Vivienne Westwood and Roksanda Ilincic, alongside newly established talents Emilia Wickstead, Holly Fulton and Jackie JS Lee and future star Sadie Williams. Collectively they have demonstrated unequivocally that fashion is not only a leading creative industry but also a serious cultural force. Their creativity, skill and ingenuity is extraordinary.

Our job at the British Fashion Council is to support and promote the UK's fashion talent on the world stage and to showcase that talent through London Fashion Week, London Collections Men and the annual British Fashion Awards. Fashion is a significant contributor to our economy, generating £26 billion a year but it also shapes our identity and contributes to our cultural life. So on behalf of the British Fashion Council I am delighted to support *Fashion & Freedom* both in my capacity as CEO and also on a more personal note, as a born and bred Mancunian!

Caroline Rush CBE, CEO British Fashion Council

Acknowledgements

14-18 NOW and Manchester City Galleries would like to thank:

Darrell Vydelingum, Creative Director of *Fashion & Freedom*, for his vision in conceiving this ambitious and ground-breaking project and his tenacious energy in realising all its strands. Jenna Rossi-Camus has produced the project and brought her vast knowledge of historic and contemporary fashion, ably assisted by Laura Thornley.

We are indebted to the designers Holly Fulton, Jackie JS Lee, Roksanda Ilincic, Vivienne Westwood, Emilia Wickstead and Sadie Williams for their creative responses to the brief and thank their teams. We are grateful to Luke Snellin for his stunning new film *first* and to James Eden and Nick Ashley from Private White V.C. who collaborated on the costumes. We are delighted to have the involvement of SHOWstudio and thank Nick and Charlotte Knight, Riana Casson and their commissioned creative teams Rei Nadal, Phoebe English, George Harvey, Gareth Pugh, Marie Schuller and Craig Green.

We are thrilled to include the next generation of fashion talent: the students from Leeds College of Art, London College of Fashion, Manchester School of Art, University of Salford and University of Westminster who have responded to *Restriction / Release* with such creativity and energy. We are grateful to the course leaders from each of the universities respectively who included the project within their curriculum, Paul Luke, John Lau, Louise Adkins, Bashir Aswat, and Andrew Groves and to Frances Corner, Head of London College of Fashion. We also extend our thanks to filmmaker Maria Gabriella Ruban, and cameraman Ben Jones, who documented the process.

Thanks to Sarah Nicol and Leicestershire County Council Museum Service, Symington Collection for the loan of their corsets. Our huge appreciation goes to Caroline Rush at the British Fashion Council and Justine Simons from the Mayor of London's Office for their support and to The Pankhurst Centre. Thanks to Bolton & Quinn, Creative Tourist, The Cogency and Modern Designers for their work on press, marketing and the campaign and exhibition design. Photographers Layla Sailor and Jez Tozer, with stylist Kim Howells, have produced stunning images for the campaign, exhibition and this publication, which has been beautifully designed by Alan Ward.

Without the generous support of the Department of Culture, Media and Sport, Arts Council England and the Heritage Lottery Fund, this project would not have been realised and we also thank La Rosa for sponsorship of the beautiful mannequins, Farrow & Ball for the exhibition colour scheme and Ocean for the provision of outdoor screens. Our sincere thanks also to MT Rainey, Kate Nelson Best and Rosie Hytner for all their support. Finally, thanks to the excellent teams at Manchester City Galleries and 14-18 NOW.

Creative Team

Creative Director	Darrell Vydelingum
Producer and Curator	Jenna Rossi-Camus
Project Co-ordinator	Laura Thornley
Exhibition Design	Modern Designers
Marketing	Creative Tourist
Photography	Jez Tozer cover, pp. 4-5, 32, 35, 37, 39, 41, 43, 45, 98-99
	Layla Sailor inner front and back cover, pp. 6, 20-27, 49, 51, 55, 57, 59, 60, 61, 63, 65, 69, 71, 73, 75, 77, 79, 81, 97
	Nick Knight pp. 92-93
Documentary film	Maria Gabriella Ruban
Publication Editors	Natasha Howes and Jenna Rossi-Camus
Additional catalogue texts	Jenna Rossi-Camus
Publication	Axis Graphic Design
Printed by	Cambrian Printers

Photography Shoots

Photography	Jez Tozer
Styling	Kim Howells
Model	Emily Bostock at IMG, cover, pp. 4-5, 96-97
Model	Sally Jonsson at Milk Management, pp. 32, 35, 37, 39, 41, 43, 45
Make-up	James O'Riley at Premier Hair and Make-up using M.A.C Cosmetics
Photography Assistant	David Vail
Hair	Bianca Tuovi at CLM Hair and Make-up
Styling assistant	Chantal des Vignes
Studio Assistants	Clara Lorusso, Freddie Mungo
Post Production	Jez Tozer Studio pp. 32, 35, 37, 39, 41, 43, 45
	Epilogue Inc cover pp. 4-5, 96-97
Photography	Layla Sailor
Hair and make-up	Rebecca Anderson
Photo assistant	Nikki Jalali
Models	Eleanor Davies at Boss pp. 59, 63, 71, 73, 75
	China at Boss pp. 49, 51, 65, 69, 81 inner back cover
	Natacha Meunier at Boss pp. 49, 51, 53, 55
	Lily Turnbull at IMG pp. 57, 61, 77, 79
Post Production	Catherine Day

14-18 NOW

Director	Jenny Waldman
Executive Producer	Nigel Hinds
Director of Brand and Communications	Claire Eva
General Manager	Pak Ling Wan
Producer	Sud Basu
Head of Development	Katie Cross
Development Manager	Alice Boff
Press and Communications	Bolton & Quinn
Marketing	The Cogency
Learning & Education	Gemma Clarke, Erin Barnes
Talks	Phoebe Greenwood
Evaluation	Morris Hargreaves Macintyre

Manchester City Galleries

Director	Dr Maria Balshaw
Deputy Director	Amanda Wallace
Senior Curator	Natasha Howes
Costume Curator	Dr Miles Lambert
Textile Consultant	Ann French
Dress and Textile Technician	Sarah Walton
Head of Development	Jo Beggs
Registrar	Phillippa Milner
Collections and Assets Assistant	Bev Hogg
Principal Operations Manager	Catriona Morgan
AV technician	Shamus Dawes
Campaigns Manager	Catherine Ryan
Web Manager	Martin Grimes
Learning Team	Ruth Edson, Meg Parnell, Jo Davies, Emma Carroll, Jess Wild, Sarah Marsh
Exhibition Intern	Julie Kristensen

Published by Manchester Art Gallery and 14-18 NOW
on the occasion of
Fashion & Freedom
13 May – 27 November 2016

www.fashionandfreedom.org

ISBN 978-0-901673-94-7

Manchester Art Gallery
Mosley Street
Manchester
M2 3JL
www.manchesterartgallery.org

14-18 NOW
Imperial War Museum
Lambeth Road
London
SE1 6HZ
www.14-18NOW.org.uk

Cover: **William R. Howell-Jackson** *Christabel* 2015
Inner cover front: **G. Worth** *Afternoon dress* 1907-9 (detail)
Inner cover back: **Joana Almagro Bustalino** *Women Voters: Conquer Freedom* 2016

EXCAT